# Who Is
# Caitlin Clark?

# Who Is Caitlin Clark?

by Meri-Jo Borzilleri

illustrated by Gregory Copeland

Penguin Workshop

Dedicated to my parents, Judy and Bill, who always knew how important it was for me to play—and for all the times they joined me—MJB

PENGUIN WORKSHOP
An imprint of Penguin Random House LLC
1745 Broadway, New York, New York 10019

First published in the United States of America by Penguin Workshop,
an imprint of Penguin Random House LLC, 2025

Visit us online at penguinrandomhouse.com.

Library of Congress Cataloging-in-Publication Data is available.

Printed in the United States of America

ISBN 9798217049172 (paperback)          10 9 8 7 6 5 4 3 2   CJKW
ISBN 9798217049189 (library binding)     10 9 8 7 6 5 4 3 2 1 CJKW

The publisher does not have any control over and does not assume any responsibility for author or third-party websites or their content.

# Contents

# Who Is Caitlin Clark?

On March 3, 2024, Caitlin Clark stood at the free-throw line and on the brink of history.

With a well-practiced flick of her wrist, she sent the basketball in a graceful arc toward the hoop. It rippled through the net. Good!

Then she did it again. This time, the shot was so perfect, the net barely moved. *Swish!*

In that moment, Caitlin became the highest scorer in National Collegiate Athletic Association (NCAA) Division I history, across both women and men. She broke "Pistol Pete" Maravich's record of 3,667 points, set in 1970—a record that many thought would never be broken, much less by a woman. There were 14,998 fans in the sold-out crowd at Carver-Hawkeye Arena. Millions more watched on TV.

Caitlin wasn't nervous taking the shot, even though the spotlight had been on her for months in anticipation of this moment. In fact, she wasn't even thinking about the record. Caitlin's free throw was as routine as it gets. She had made the same shot thousands of times, practicing in her driveway as a kid, playing in high school, and playing for the University of Iowa.

But this game was anything but routine. The attention Caitlin got in the run-up to the record was extraordinary. Even people who did not follow basketball were buzzing about Caitlin. Her trademark "logo threes"—three-pointers made from near mid-court where the school logo was printed—had made her a household name, like male basketball icons LeBron James and Stephen Curry.

From that moment on, Caitlin had cemented herself in history. She'd only continue to grow more popular, and she'd continue to break records as she debuted in the Women's National Basketball Association (WNBA) as a professional player.

Now, Caitlin is one of the most beloved athletes in the world—but twenty years ago she had just been a little girl who wanted to play basketball with her brothers.

# CHAPTER 1
## Little Caitlin

Caitlin Clark was born on January 22, 2002, in West Des Moines, Iowa, to Brent Clark and Anne Nizzi-Clark. Caitlin grew up as the middle child of two brothers, Blake and Colin, in a competitive family that loved playing and watching sports.

Brent had played basketball and baseball at Iowa's Simpson College. Blake, Caitlin's older brother, was the quarterback for Iowa State's football team. Caitlin is especially close to her older cousin Audrey Faber, who played basketball for Creighton University and later became a girls' basketball coach at Dowling Catholic High School, where Caitlin would eventually go to school.

Caitlin's childhood was full of activities, mostly sports. She played basketball, soccer, volleyball, tennis, softball, and golf. She didn't like things like video games—if she wasn't playing a sport, she'd rather hit a tennis ball against the wall or throw a football around.

She had a competitive spirit even outside of sports. If there was a school math contest in first grade, Caitlin wanted to win. When her older brother Blake first rode his bike without training wheels, four-year-old Caitlin was determined to do it, too.

Caitlin and her brothers were constantly competing against one another. Once, playing basketball in the basement, she missed a shot and, in frustration, shoved Colin into a wall. He hit his head and needed stitches. Caitlin was apologetic, but Colin wasn't mad at her—he understood his sister wasn't being a bully or trying to hurt him. She was just competitive like him.

When Caitlin was around five, her parents put her in a nearby boys' basketball league where her dad was the coach. Right away, people noticed her, and not just because she was the only girl. She was also the best player on the team! Caitlin played in the league from kindergarten to third grade. She would make long shots that no one else could. Teammates knew that if they got the ball to Caitlin, she would probably score. The boys on opposing teams knew she was the one to stop.

By second grade, Caitlin was the league's most valuable player (MVP). Her parents put up a hoop above the garage and eventually had to dig up grass to extend the driveway because Caitlin wanted to shoot from farther and farther back.

Basketball wasn't Caitlin's only sport. She liked soccer, too. When she was eleven and in a youth league tournament final, she asked her coach if she could shoot from the field's center circle on a kickoff following a goal. The coach said yes. Caitlin hatched the plan with teammates, one of whom had to touch the ball first. Then, Caitlin took a running start and swung her foot. The kick sailed toward the net, catching the goalkeeper by surprise and scoring a goal! The coach said later this showed how, even at a young age, Caitlin was different—she could do things most kids could not, and saw opportunities that others might not.

Still, basketball remained Caitlin's favorite. She liked watching college and professional games. The closest WNBA team to the Clarks was the Minnesota Lynx in Minneapolis, a four-hour drive away. Caitlin loved watching the Lynx play. They won four WNBA championships while she was growing up. Caitlin especially liked all-star Maya Moore, the forward who had played for Caitlin's favorite college team—the University of Connecticut—before turning pro. Once, Caitlin and her dad drove to Minneapolis for a game when Caitlin was twelve. After the game, as fans and players mixed on court, Caitlin ran up to Maya. When Caitlin got to her, she realized she didn't have a phone to take a photo. So Caitlin just gave her a big hug. Maya hugged her back. The moment lasted only about ten seconds but stayed with Caitlin forever.

As Caitlin continued playing basketball, she kept getting better and better. When she was in sixth grade, she started to play on an all-girls team in the All Iowa Attack program, a well-known league. After just one year, she was good enough to compete with fourteen-year-olds while she herself was only twelve. By the time she was fourteen, she was playing against girls who were seventeen.

When Caitlin was in seventh and eighth grade, college coaches around the country were noticing her. They began sending Caitlin recruiting letters, asking her to play for their teams—even though she hadn't even started high school yet. Caitlin's parents tried to shield her from all the attention because they didn't want her to feel pressured at such a young age. They would send Blake ahead to open the mail so Caitlin wouldn't see all of it.

But the attention would only grow: Caitlin Clark, basketball superstar, was about to enter high school.

# CHAPTER 2
# High School Ball

Caitlin's college decision had to wait. High school basketball had begun, and her hoops game continued to grow.

During her first year at Dowling Catholic, a private school, Caitlin averaged 15.3 points, 4.7 assists, and 2.3 steals per game and was named to the Class 5A all-state third team, which meant Caitlin was among the state's top fifteen players. This was rare for a freshman—most players to receive this honor were seniors.

The summer after her freshman year, something even bigger happened—the national team called fifteen-year-old Caitlin! USA Basketball invited her to Colorado to try out for the under-sixteen national team that would play a tournament in Buenos Aires, Argentina. Competition was fierce for the twelve spots on the team. Caitlin wanted to be as ready as she could. Before tryouts, she and her high school coach practiced shooting from the international three-point line, which was farther out. Caitlin took it very seriously and practiced while wearing a special mask that made her feel like she was at Colorado's high altitude, where breathing is more difficult for athletes.

When she made the team, Caitlin was thrilled.

But a year later, she did not make the under-seventeen team. Caitlin used it to motivate herself and was soon named the Gatorade National Player of the Year after her junior year season. Caitlin eventually won World Cup gold medals with the under-nineteen team in 2019 and 2021. She was even named MVP of the tournament.

In high school, Caitlin kept dazzling coaches. She continued to play soccer during her freshman and sophomore years. Her soccer coaches said that she could have played at the national level in that sport if she had wanted to. A tall striker with a powerful shot, Caitlin scored a remarkable twenty-six goals in just six games and was the only freshman named first-team all-state. Like in basketball, her height—almost six feet tall—combined with her strength made her an uncommon talent. Caitlin found that soccer made her basketball game even better. It trained her to create room for herself in crowded spaces so she could get passes from teammates. It also helped her develop her skill at making amazing passes on the basketball court. Caitlin didn't practice passing against a wall to get better like a lot of other players do. She practiced by playing both basketball and soccer, which helped her understand angles.

After sophomore year, Caitlin quit soccer to put all her effort into basketball. In one game her junior year, she scored a remarkable sixty points, one point short of the state record. She hit a state-record thirteen out of seventeen attempted three-pointers. As a joke, opposing schools' students chanted "Overrated!" at her during games. Caitlin would just laugh. After the game, they'd ask for her autograph.

It wasn't always easy being so good. Caitlin had a fire that sometimes worked against her. She'd get frustrated by her teammates who couldn't always handle her passes. Even though she piled up big scoring and rebounding numbers, it didn't always mean her team would win. Dowling Catholic did not win a state title in the four years Caitlin played, but that didn't stop college coaches from wanting Caitlin on their team. Caitlin was rated the number four prospect in the nation in girls' basketball. She dreamed of playing for the University of Connecticut, like Maya Moore. Coaches from other big teams would come watch Caitlin play. But Connecticut's head coach, Geno Auriemma, did not show interest, so Caitlin had to set her sights elsewhere.

After all those years, letters, and visits by coaches, Caitlin narrowed her choices to the University of Notre Dame, the University of Iowa, and Iowa State University. Finally, she decided on Notre Dame. She called the head coach, Muffet McGraw, and told her she'd come. But the more Caitlin thought, the more she believed she had made the wrong decision. What she really wanted was to play for the University of Iowa. Caitlin's mom loved Notre Dame, and Caitlin was worried about disappointing her by not choosing that school. But this had to be what Caitlin wanted, not what she thought her mom wanted . . . so it had to be the University of Iowa.

That meant that Caitlin had to call Muffet McGraw and tell her she had changed her mind. Caitlin dreaded making the call. She eventually gained the courage to do it. Muffet understood, and Caitlin was relieved. Then Caitlin called Iowa's head coach, Lisa Bluder, who was overjoyed to have Caitlin on the team.

The University of Iowa is located in Iowa City, just a two-hour drive from Caitlin's home. She was happy to be close to her family.

Caitlin's other reason for choosing Iowa was a far bolder one. She wanted to bring the team to the best of women's collegiate basketball: the semifinals of the national tournament, famously known as the NCAA Final Four. Iowa had done it only once before. That was in 1993—nine years before Caitlin was born. Caitlin was determined to lead Iowa to new heights.

# CHAPTER 3
## College Stardom

The Caitlin Clark era at the University of Iowa began November 25, 2020, in front of many empty seats. Because of restrictions from the COVID-19 pandemic, not many fans saw Iowa's 96–81 victory over Northern Iowa at Iowa's Carver-Hawkeye Arena.

That didn't matter to Caitlin. She scored twenty-seven points in her first college game, more than anyone else on the court. She also had eight rebounds and four assists, giving the small crowd a glimpse of what was to come.

By the time Caitlin's first season was over, she led the nation in scoring—averaging 26.6 points per game. Her season totals in points, assists, field goals (baskets made outside of free throws), and three-pointers led all NCAA Division I women. She became the first freshman to win the Dawn Staley Award, presented to the best NCAA women's Division I point guard.

The season ended without a trip to the semifinals, but Caitlin persisted. Iowa reached the NCAA tournament's Sweet 16, just two wins away from the Final Four. The Hawkeyes lost, 92–72, to the University of Connecticut, the team that did not recruit Caitlin. After the game, coach Geno Auriemma sought out Caitlin to congratulate her for her play and her impact on women's basketball. He and many others sensed Iowa and Caitlin were on the verge of something big.

That summer, Caitlin tried out for Team USA's under-nineteen team. Caitlin played well, but her tryout team had lost all its scrimmages (practice games). After tryouts were over, Coach Cori Close asked Caitlin an important question: Did she want to be a player who piled up a lot of big stats or did she want her team to *win*?

Caitlin wanted to win. She made the team and won gold in Hungary. Caitlin was named tournament MVP. She learned that scoring a lot of points or grabbing a lot of rebounds is one thing, but getting everyone involved helps a team win.

In order to do that, Caitlin had to learn to trust her teammates. In high school, teammates weren't as intense about the sport as Caitlin. In college, Caitlin found her people—teammates who committed their whole lives to basketball like she did.

But Caitlin demanded the best from herself, and from them, not only in games but in practices. She could be impatient with teammates who didn't expect a pass from her or couldn't anticipate when to get open. It was frustrating for everyone. Caitlin would have outbursts during practice when she or someone else made a mistake. She would sometimes yell, spin around, or scowl, stressing out her teammates and lowering their confidence. Coaches had to figure out a way to keep the whole team working as a unit.

The coaches put together a video of nothing but Caitlin's body language to help her see how she was affecting the team and her own play. If Iowa was to get to the Final Four, Caitlin would have to learn to control her emotions without losing her desire to win.

Her sophomore year, Caitlin's skills got better and better. She attracted attention when she had back-to-back thirty-point triple-double games, the first Division I player, man or woman, to ever do so.

Then came February 6, 2022, and a game against Michigan. Caitlin excelled, scoring forty-six points in a 98–90 loss. Caitlin scored twenty-five points in the fourth quarter alone. Several of Caitlin's shots came from just past half-court, a lot farther from the basket than the three-point line. Social media started buzzing about the Iowa player who made shots from incredible distances.

By the end of the season, Caitlin was named the conference player of the year, which was unusual for someone in only their second year of college basketball. She was the first person to win back-to-back Dawn Staley Awards. She averaged twenty-seven points, eight rebounds, and eight assists per game, becoming the first woman in history to lead the NCAA Division I in points and assists per game. Usually, a player will lead in one or the other. Leading in points and assists meant Caitlin scored more than anyone but was also the best in women's college basketball at helping her teammates score.

Yet when it came to the NCAA tournament, Iowa experienced a big disappointment. They lost in the second round to underdog Creighton, 64–62. Iowa and Caitlin had just two seasons left to make good on her promise to reach the Final Four.

Then, it happened. Caitlin's junior year was a

breakthrough season. In the NCAA tournament, Caitlin's long-distance three-point shots, along with her thread-the-needle passes, were gaining attention around the country. In a nationally televised Elite Eight game (the round before the Final Four), Caitlin scored a triple-double that was mind-boggling—forty-one points, twelve assists, and ten rebounds. Iowa beat Louisville, 97–83, to advance to the Final Four. Caitlin had done it!

During the tournament, Caitlin passed the nine-hundred-point and three-hundred-assist mark in a season, the first player in men's or women's tournament history to do so.

Big names were paying attention—LeBron James, Magic Johnson, Billie Jean King, and others took to social media to express their admiration for Caitlin.

The next game—the semifinal against the University of South Carolina—would be the biggest challenge yet. They were the nation's top team and the defending national champions.

But Caitlin and her team pulled off a surprise win—77–73! Caitlin had forty-one points, eight assists, and six rebounds. She became the first player in tournament history to record back-to-back forty-point games. By now, Caitlin had become such a draw that TV ratings skyrocketed—averaging 5.5 million viewers.

Not only had Caitlin helped bring Iowa to the Final Four, but now they would play in the finals for the first time in their team's history. The Hawkeyes faced Louisiana State (LSU) in a showdown between two of college basketball's big stars, Caitlin and LSU's Angel Reese. A sellout crowd of 19,482 spectators packed the American Airlines Center in Dallas, Texas. But despite Caitlin's thirty points, including eight three-pointers, Iowa lost to LSU, 102–85. A record 9.9 million watched on TV.

# CHAPTER 4
## Senior Season

As her senior year began, Caitlin's popularity soared. Iowa sold out of season tickets before the season even started. She was so well-known that the Iowa State Fair had a life-size statue of her made of butter, an honor bestowed on famous Iowans.

Caitlin Clark butter sculpture

Her name got so big that the university held an exhibition game in the school's football stadium to try to break the single-game attendance record for women's basketball. It worked, with a crowd of 55,646 crushing the previous mark of 29,619.

Caitlin was closing in on other big numbers—ones that would cement her place in college basketball history. On February 15, 2024, she scored a career-high forty-nine points, with thirteen assists, to become the women's career NCAA Division I scoring leader in dramatic fashion when she hit a huge three-pointer in a win against Michigan to pass Kelsey Plum's record of 3,527 points, set in 2017.

Fewer than two weeks later, she passed Lynette Woodard's all-time major college women's mark of 3,649 points, set from 1977 to 1981, prior to women's sports joining the NCAA.

But the biggest record of them all was still to

come. On March 3, 2024—Caitlin's final game of the regular season in her final year of college basketball—the superstar calmly sank two free throws to surpass the all-time NCAA Division I collegiate career scoring record for men and women set by "Pistol Pete" Maravich. He had scored 3,667 points between 1967 and 1970.

Before the game, held on Senior Night, Maya Moore paid Caitlin a surprise visit near the Hawkeye locker room. Caitlin couldn't believe her idol was standing in front of her! They hugged, just as they had that memorable day years before when ten-year-old Caitlin ran across the court to her. It was the most vivid basketball memory Caitlin had growing up. Back then, she had been a little kid looking up to Maya. Now she and Maya saw each other at eye-level.

After Senior Night, Iowa went on to win the Big Ten Conference tournament, and Caitlin blew past Stephen Curry and Darius McGhee's record for most three-pointers in a season, man or woman. The two men had each made 162 three-pointers in a single season . . . Caitlin would go on to end her season with a grand total of 201.

In the 2024 NCAA tournament, Caitlin continued to set tournament and college records— her nine three-pointers in the Elite Eight win over

LSU helped her become the all-time leader in collegiate career threes—but she had her eye on a bigger prize: a first-time national championship for Iowa. She helped Iowa beat Connecticut and its star, Paige Bueckers, in the Final Four to reach the title game for a second-straight season. This time, they'd play South Carolina.

South Carolina and its head coach, Dawn Staley, were ready. Caitlin started hot, scoring eighteen points in the first quarter, the most by a player in a single quarter in a national championship game. But South Carolina, led by big, agile center Kamilla Cardoso, proved too much for the Hawkeyes. South Carolina won, 87–75, finishing their season undefeated. Caitlin would end her college career with two Final Fours and two NCAA Finals . . . but no championship.

But the ultimate champion at the end of the day was women's college basketball. Thanks to Caitlin and players like Cardoso, Bueckers, and Reese, more people were watching women's college basketball than ever before. On TV, the title game averaged a jaw-dropping 18.9 million viewers. This was the first time that the women's championship drew more viewers than the men's championship, which averaged 14.8 million viewers.

The game was watched more than many important professional sports games—more than any of the 2023 baseball World Series games or any of the five games of the 2023 NBA Finals.

During her victory speech after the NCAA championship, South Carolina coach Dawn Staley called Caitlin one of college basketball's GOATs (greatest of all time) and took the unusual step of thanking Caitlin, the opposing team's star, for lifting women's basketball to new heights.

Caitlin finished her four-year college career with a record 3,951 points—averaging close to 1,000 points per season! Her 1,144 assists rank third in NCAA women's basketball history.

Because of the pandemic affecting sports her freshman year, Caitlin had been eligible to play college basketball an extra, fifth year. But she decided not to. Instead, she wanted to enter the WNBA draft and officially become a professional player.

# CHAPTER 5
## The Caitlin Clark Effect

On April 15, 2024, WNBA draft day, Caitlin was overwhelmed. The WNBA draft is when all the professional teams select their new players. In the week leading up to this event, Caitlin was seemingly everywhere.

Caitlin was treated like a movie star, with hair and makeup people tending to her before arriving at the draft in a white satin skirt, shirt, and mesh top embroidered with rhinestones. Her outfit was designed by the famous fashion company Prada. It was rare for Caitlin to wear anything like that.

This was a big day. Caitlin and her family were all about to officially find out where she'd play professionally.

The Indiana Fever took Caitlin as the draft's first pick. This was expected because Indiana had first pick of the new players, and everyone wanted Caitlin on their team.

Caitlin had made a big splash in New York.

Two days before the draft even happened, she had been invited to appear on the historic comedy show *Saturday Night Live*. When she appeared onstage, the crowd went wild. Not many athletes are invited on the show, and even fewer are met with such excitement.

A term emerged for the impact Caitlin was having on the sport of women's basketball: the Caitlin Clark Effect. The kind of recognition Caitlin got for her play led to national TV commercials, billboards with her face on them, sold-out jerseys, and crowds of fans desperate to catch a glimpse of her wherever she went.

Caitlin changed the way many people viewed women's basketball. Before Caitlin, people hardly ever saw the value of promoting women's sports. Now, popular new players like Caitlin, Angel Reese, Paige Bueckers, Cameron Brink, and Kamilla Cardoso gave them a reason to.

Caitlin's first game with the Indiana Fever

was a sellout because fans wanted to see her play. Within an hour after she was chosen at the WNBA draft, her jersey was sold out in most sizes.

Fans weren't just showing up in person— Caitlin's first game with the Fever drew the biggest ESPN TV rating in history for a WNBA game, with 2.1 million watching. A month later, more tuned in when the Fever played against Angel Reese and the Chicago Sky—2.3 million watched on CBS.

Before 2024, it was rare for the WNBA to draw one million TV viewers for a game. It hadn't happened since 2008. But at the 2024 season's midway point, more than a dozen game telecasts had hit that mark.

Caitlin had become one of the biggest draws in women's sports. No WNBA rookie had generated the excitement Clark did. Midway through her first season, the twelve highest-rated games were all Indiana Fever games.

Just like in college, the Clark Effect had lifted up other teams, too. The Las Vegas Aces moved their July game against Indiana from their home arena, which had twelve thousand seats, to T-Mobile Arena's eighteen-thousand-seat venue.

Though the Fever had not won a WNBA title since 2012, Caitlin was thrilled to be picked by them in the draft. Indianapolis—where the Fever played—was an eight-hour drive from her hometown.

Even though she was happy to be playing professionally, not everything was going smoothly for Caitlin. Some WNBA superstars, like Diana Taurasi and Breanna Stewart, along with others who had worked hard in the league for years, resented the fact that a rookie had already gotten so much attention before she had even played one professional game. Caitlin would have to prove that she was worth the hype she had around her.

In her first game as a pro, Caitlin had a rough start. She scored twenty points but committed a record-breaking ten turnovers. Turnovers are when a player mistakenly gives the ball to the other team, usually through a bad pass. This was not a good record to break.

She also had to tolerate some bruising and sometimes unfair play. Once, during a game, another player shoved her to the floor, even though the ball was not even in play. Still, Caitlin had to remain focused on the game and avoid being distracted by the drama other players were attempting to create.

Soon into the season, Caitlin had adjusted to professional basketball, earning the respect of most players who had treated her unfairly earlier. She led the WNBA in assists and was in the top fifteen in points and steals. However, she also led the league in turnovers and technical fouls, so she still had a lot of growing to do.

Halfway through the WNBA season, Caitlin erased any doubts people had about her skills. She became the fastest player, rookie or not, to reach 350 points and 150 assists to start a WNBA season. She set the WNBA single-game record for assists (nineteen) and had the first triple-double by a rookie in league history. At the end of the 2024 season, Caitlin was named the WNBA Rookie of the Year.

By the time Caitlin turned pro, she was making more than $3 million through sponsorships for clothing, gear, insurance companies, grocery stores, and more. Her WNBA salary, though, was only $76,535, the limit for rookies. The NBA's top draft pick, San Antonio Spurs star Victor Wembanyama, was given nearly $12.2 million. To many, this shows how women's basketball still has a long way to go to reach equality.

Only time will tell if Caitlin will be able to bring success to the Indiana Fever the way she did with the University of Iowa, but this much is certain: The determined kid who loved hitting long shots in her driveway is now a model for young girls around the country. Caitlin made her mark by bringing unprecedented attention to not only women's basketball but also women's sports. Her future is bright . . . and she's just getting started.

# History of the Women's National Basketball Association

The Women's National Basketball Association (WNBA) started play in June 1997. Some of the first players were members of the United States' iconic 1996 Olympic team, such as Lisa Leslie, Dawn Staley, Cynthia Cooper, Rebecca Lobo, and Sheryl Swoopes.

The WNBA started with eight teams. Today, there are twelve. Iconic recent players include Diana Taurasi, Sue Bird, Candace Parker, Maya Moore, and Tina Charles. In 2013, the WNBA draft was televised for the first time in prime time, thanks to excitement around future stars Brittney Griner, Elena Delle Donne, and Skylar Diggins. In 2024, millions of viewers tuned in to watch WNBA games when new fans came to watch superstar rookies Caitlin Clark and Angel Reese.

# Timeline of Caitlin Clark's Life

**2002** — Caitlin Clark is born in West Des Moines, Iowa

**2007** — Begins playing basketball at age five

— Joins a boys' recreational league

**2013** — Joins All Iowa Attack

**2017** — Scores twenty-three goals as a freshman soccer player

**2019** — Scores a record sixty points for Dowling Catholic in beating Mason City

— Sets the single-game record for three-pointers with thirteen

**2020** — Makes University of Iowa debut with twenty-seven points, eight rebounds, and four assists

**2021** — Becomes first freshman to win the Dawn Staley Award, honoring the best NCAA women's Division I guard

**2022** — First player in NCAA history, man or woman, to record back-to-back triple-doubles

**2023** — Helps Iowa set women's basketball attendance record of 55,646 against DePaul at Kinnick Stadium, Iowa's football stadium

**2024** — Breaks all-time NCAA Division I career scoring record set by Pete Maravich

— Drafted number one by the WNBA Indiana Fever

— Wins WNBA Rookie of the Year award

# Timeline of the World

| | |
|---|---|
| 2002 | The 2002 Winter Olympics take place in Salt Lake City |
| 2004 | Harvard student Mark Zuckerberg launches Facebook |
| 2005 | Hurricane Katrina devastates the US Gulf Coast |
| 2007 | Apple releases its first iPhone, priced at $499 |
| 2009 | Barack Obama is sworn in as the first African American president |
| 2011 | Al-Qaeda founder Osama bin Laden, responsible for the September 11 attacks, is killed by US Navy SEALs |
| 2012 | "Gangnam Style" becomes first YouTube video in history to reach one billion views |
| 2014 | Pakistani activist Malala Yousafzai, seventeen, becomes youngest recipient of the Nobel Prize for supporting children's rights to education |
| 2017 | More than five million people in more than six hundred marches globally protest for women's rights |
| 2020 | COVID-19 is declared a pandemic by the World Health Organization |
| 2023 | With 1.3 billion people, India surpasses China to become the world's most populous country |

# Bibliography

Bachman, Rachel, and Jared Diamond. "Before Caitlin Clark
Dominated Women's Basketball, She Dominated These Boys."
*Wall Street Journal*. March 27, 2024. https://www.wsj.com/
sports/basketball/caitlin-clark-iowa-march-madness-
34658e46.

Bachman, Rachel. "Caitlin Clark Didn't Just Grow the WNBA's
Audience—She Also Changed It." *Wall Street Journal*. July 22,
2024. https://www.wsj.com/sports/basketball/caitlin-clark-
wnba-ratings-392cffc9.

"Caitlin Clark's Fever Jersey Sells Out Most Sizes One Hour After
Being Drafted." *Fox Sports*. April 16, 2024. https://www.
foxsports.com/stories/wnba/caitlin-clarks-fever-jersey-
mostly-sold-out-just-one-hour-after-being-drafted.

*Full Court Press*. Streaming series. ESPN+. Summer 2024. https://
www.espn.com/watch/series/7a8c271f-8e83-4f5f-8dfe-
e950c8b2ae09/full-court-press/.

Golliver, Ben. "Feared and Loved, Iowa's Caitlin Clark Is Taking
Women's Basketball by Storm." *Washington Post*. March 14,
2023. https://www.washingtonpost.com/sports/2023/03/14/
caitlin-clark-iowa-ncaa-tournament/.

Leistikow, Chad. "Why Iowa Basketball's Caitlin Clark Could Have Been a Superstar in Soccer, Too." *Hawk Central*. February 8, 2024. https://www.hawkcentral.com/story/sports/college/iowa/basketball-women/2024/02/08/iowa-womens-basketball-caitlin-clark-ncaa-scoring-record-soccer-dowling-catholic-ncaa/72339992007/.

Leuzzi, John. "Caitlin Clark Scoring Record: What Iowa Star Said Moments After Passing Pete Maravich." *USA Today Network*. March 3, 2024. https://www.hawkcentral.com/story/sports/college/iowa/basketball-women/2024/03/03/caitlin-clark-ncaa-all-time-leading-scorer-iowa-hawkeyes-womens-basketball-fox-sports/72831724007/.

Pickman, Ben. "From Iowa Attack to Final Four: Where Caitlin Clark and Several Hawkeyes Started." *New York Times*. March 30, 2023. https://www.nytimes.com/athletic/4363721/2023/03/30/caitlin-clark-iowa-attack/.

Rosen, Karen. "From West Des Moines . . ." *Caitlin Clark, The Future of Basketball*. Accelerate360 Media. June 2024.

Schnell, Lindsay. "Caitlin Clark, Maya Moore and a 10-Second Interaction that Changed Clark's Life." *USA Today*. May 1, 2024. https://www.usatoday.com/story/sports/wnba/2024/05/01/caitlin-clark-maya-moore-10-second-interaction/73378001007/.

Thompson, Wright. "Finding Peace in the Process." *ESPN*. March 20, 2024. https://www.espn.com/womens-college-basketball/story/_/id/39740282/caitlin-clark-iowa-2024-ncaa-women-basketball-tournament-ready-march.

Villa, Walter. "After a Measured Approach to Trials, Recruit Caitlin Clark Riding High with USA Basketball." *ESPN*. May 30, 2017. https://www.espn.com/espnw/sports/story/_/id/19577932/dowling-catholic-caitlin-clark-rides-athleticism-usa-basketball-roster-spot-fiba-americas-argentina.